BOOK OF
OMENS

BOOK OF OMENS

RENATO BETTIO

Halo
PUBLISHING
INTERNATIONAL

Halo Publishing International
7550 WIH-10 #800, PMB 2069,
San Antonio, TX 78229

First Edition, June 2024
ISBN: 978-1-63765-625-9
Library of Congress Control Number: 2024911358

Halo Publishing International is a self-publishing company that publishes adult fiction and non-fiction, children's literature, self-help, spiritual, and faith-based books. We continually strive to help authors reach their publishing goals and provide many different services that help them do so. We do not publish books that are deemed to be politically, religiously, or socially disrespectful, or books that are sexually provocative, including erotica. Halo reserves the right to refuse publication of any manuscript if it is deemed not to be in line with our principles. Do you have a book idea you would like us to consider publishing? Please visit www.halopublishing.com for more information.

Contents

Prologue

Somewhere along the way that took me here, an unease had to be born, the desire to have the mind's empire endure in the written, understandable word. For my own sake and for everyone else's.

There's this proverb, "One must write a book to remain," and it sounds unattainable. If I was to dream of one day publishing a book written by me, a stranger to the literary scene full of genius writers who changed the road for the better, or at least changed it, there had to be a good reason.

And there's a good reason for everyone: believing that somehow, we can make a difference for the people, our people, most of all the forgotten, those we call "the poor," those who endure eternal abuse at the hand of those elected to protect them and make a way through the wasteland so we can all "move forward."

Let this little introduction be my presentation in your uneasy eyes.

I am grateful for your kindness and your presence.

Renato Bettio

Book
of Omens

Paco Luna

For the simple crime of stealing a bicycle, Paco Luna found himself in Usulután, in prison. Coincidentally, as Paco's cell's metallic gate was being opened, in a far-off country, a far more opulent gate opened, too. The gate, framed in wood and bronze, was made of engraved crystal and stood in a street in Paris, closing a mansion. This gate was opening for a thief who was just like any thief that has ever walked our earth; this one had just bought the property. His name was being mentioned in every newspaper, for his crimes were well-known by the nation: he stole no less than twenty million dollars from the meager resources of the country when he was the National Clean Water Services Manager. He decided to move to Paris and lead a respectable life in a wonderful city. Mr. Concha—that was his name— did not have a respectable thing about his character. Blatant in his actions, he was simply a shameless thief.

Paco Luna knew about the thefts, just as everybody else knew about them. This gave him the boldness to throw the incomparably unjust nature of what was being done to him in the jailer's faces: "How is it that I'm being thrown in *chirona* for stealing an old bicycle just to be able to get to my construction job when Mr. Concha is being bothered by no one after pocketing twenty million dollars?"

The jailers considered this unnecessary to answer and pushed him into his cell, where five other men, condemned for God-knows-what other crimes, were being held.

Paco showed up on the streets of town on no particular day, suddenly, as did all the others who had come running away from the war. As many of them, Paco was born alone, over a naked land, with no one to knot his umbilicus: no parents, no welcome, no love, surrounded by unbelievable misery and eternal hunger; grabbing at any morsel that would serve him as nourishment.

He had a passed-over soul, a hardened heart with no regrets, a mind closed to anything that wasn't violence; he had been seen hitting children just for the pleasure of watching them cry. Hunger, as happened to Don Quixote, had dried up his brain. His limited intelligence wouldn't allow him to differentiate the essential from the extemporaneous; he lived in the moment, and each moment led him to misfortune. Daily drugs and alcohol took him to a brighter world in which he was the main character of heroic scenes that always ended in triumph. He lived in the filthy room of a filthy inn alongside cockroaches and other vermin but preferred to sleep on the street. He would beg for anything from anyone who happened to be passing by the town streets and got mad when nothing was given to him. This poisoned his heart further.

He got a job as a ticket collector on a bus line. These buses moved, near and far, between the town and the capital. It wasn't long before he learned to keep a part of the ticket money for himself, was found out and fired immediately. That was it. So, a friend of his, a drinking partner and *marero*, helped him get a job as a construction assistant in another town. So, as he had to walk five full kilometers to get to the neighboring town, Paco decided to steal a bicycle that had been left unattended in an alley on a Sunday market.

The owner, a baker who used the bicycle to deliver his bread to stores in town, saw Paco steal the bicycle and push it toward the street, making a path through the crowded alley by force of screams and punches. The baker chased Paco, yelling at him to stop and calling for help from anyone else to stop Paco. Paco made it to the main street and disappeared into the afternoon's crowd.

Days later, as Paco arrived in town after work, three men were waiting for him at the end of the slope of the Pumping Station that provided the entire town with water. Before he could escape, they tied his hands and threw him in the back of a pick-up truck. With two other men at his sides to stop him in case of an escape maneuver and brought him to the Usulután's prison to wait for his sentence. And that was it.

Meanwhile, Mr. Concha's life wasn't entirely going well, either. He had recently heard about the news of a new government taking over his country. Even though this government was of the same party that he was, it was desperate to gain sympathy by diminishing the impression of fraud, theft, arrogance, and nepotism that the people had over that party and therefore had redacted laws that didn't suit him. These included the extradition of him and his family in order to judge him on unlawful enrichment charges.

When he heard of this, Mr. Concha's heart stopped. "How dare they do this to me? I was always loyal to the cause," he said furiously.

He inserted lawyers, pleas, and whatever resources available to him to interfere with the extradition. France responded affirmatively and, after a few months, dispatched the order of extradition and transferred of the man and his family to the country that was to judge him for his blatant thievery of a poor country. Immediately, Mr. Concha faked a terrible illness and sent clinical analysis, reviewed and certified by great and eminent French doctors, to his country. These doctors diagnosed him with incurable illnesses that demanded no long trips if a fatal ending was to be avoided. Mr. Concha *had* to stay in Paris and in his house, in the care of expert nurses and doctors.

But as time went by, travel was again permitted for Mr. Concha, so he embarked on the painful trip back to the country where he was born and provided him with the invaluable love of a noble parent; the country that raised him inside its classrooms and smiled along with his games and happiness; that protected him with the care of a mother as he was leaving his childhood and youth in the eternal landscape of his homeland. That country, which he never called his own, had to face his perversion as it awoke inside him only hostility, mockery, and scorn. Now it would finally question him deeply enough to be pained and stripped of his honor as his soul flooded with the putrid mud that surrounded him, for "there is no lower, more criminal thing than stealing from the poor." Mr. Concha entered, by his own will, into national history as a thief. And he alone had the power to emerge from the infamy, where there are no friends, only a mirror that reflects the soul that is to follow us till the end of days.

As he arrived back on his motherland, his instinct wouldn't tremble with emotion, as he was not as a turtle or a tadpole yearning to return to the place of their birth. The gaps of his soul welcomed not even the hardest of tenderness for his race, his land, his beginning; on the contrary, his very soul despised his own blood. This very thing was what allowed him to hurt his people and leave with no remorse. As he landed, his face reflected sadness, and he needed a wheelchair to be moved directly to the prison in which he had to await sentencing.

He was valiant at his trial and sentencing. He spent nine years in jail. Not even the most despicable of criminals would go near him. When he was let out, shame obliged him to return to Paris to live with his own conscience.

Paco Luna was also processed and condemned for his theft. He spent a month in Usulután's prison and then returned to his own town to reunite with his *mara*. He was crueler in his actions against young *mareros* looking to join the ranks. He never accepted help from any family that offered to pay his way through school, to teach him to read; he sold gifted notebooks and books for almost nothing. The church offered him a daily meal in exchange for his stay at school, and Paco refused. His life trajectory was irremediably tilted towards crime, failure, and death. He once thought about joining a caravan of migrants that headed north, but he was marked by his own violence: armed groups that were forming as a defense against *maras* made a target of him.

In complicity with the *maras*, judges and governors alike made life impossible for the people; anguish and helplessness created a temerarious response. But, at the end of all things, it would be obvious that the solution required unity, a shared feeling to bring honesty into the government and open the gate to a far less miserable destiny, one that was richer and suited for a developing country that walked with pride amongst the ranks of free people.

A Quiet Afternoon

The assassination occurred at 5:20 p.m. on a February evening, a quiet month with hot days and cold nights. Ana Luisa—sixteen years old, jet-black hair, green eyes—was on her way home with a dollar-worth bag of *pan dulce* bought on the town's market.

Her house stood on an alley behind the cemetery. Ana, as to avoid taking a three-block detour, had to walk through the cemetery's gate. A five-member gang controlled the cemetery. The youngest was fourteen years old and enjoyed guarding the gate with a machine gun crossing his chest—he was known as El Hombrecito de la Metralla.

La *mara* controlled any work that could be done at the cemetery, such as the construction of niches or mausoleums. Yet not one of the members had ever worked in construction or carpentry and barely knew how to read or count, as their intelligence wouldn't allow for the absorption of new things. Lico, El Tuco, leader of the *mara*, was a cold, violent criminal. His acts included rape, theft, bribery, threats, shooting at houses full of people who couldn't afford the "security rent," the knifing of a *pandillero* that dared insult him in front of his girlfriend…

During one of the many confrontations with opposing *maras* that fought for the control of territory, the leader of one of them, El Choco Ibañez—his name gained for being blind on his left eye—threw a blow with a machete *against* Lico and so precise that he completely gashed Lico´s left hand and wrist from the forearm down. Lico spent three months at a public hospital scheming his revenge and waiting to proceed with his life of pillaging. Months later, a burned, slashed corpse was found in a ravine, tied to a *conacaste* tree. He had a nail plunged in his left eye.

Everybody understood that Lico had been the author of such savagery, but there was no persecution, no witnesses—at least not one willing to declare. And so Lico strengthened his position as head of the Mara del panteón.

The *pandilleros* knew about Ana Luisa; they had harassed her to come talk to them, and she had always evaded them. To avoid them, she walked on the other side of the cemetery's entrance, rushing through the path that led to the house where she lived with her parents.

That tragic evening, as Ana Luisa walked through the gate, the five sets of eyes followed her as she stepped down of the path at the end of the cemetery's fence in her way towards her house. They watched her disappear on the street, looked at each other, and ran for her. Luck was in their side and against Ana Luisa: there was no one on the street to intervene.

They surrounded her, and one of them covered her mouth with a dirty handkerchief as the rest lifted her up and carried her towards a small hill on the side of the road. They rushed her up the hill, then down the gorge, and the six of them disappeared towards the beginning of the night.

El Hombrecito de la Metralla had been abandoned by his parents, who incited him to rob and trick until they finally disappeared forever. He was left wandering through town, surviving on the merchants' kindness. He knew not how to read, but he did know how to hurt and fight against any aggressor. When he broke into a house, he believed was vacant, he was left with a machete slash on the face and a bullet in his left thigh, which stopped him from walking normally.

His introduction to the pandilla was violent; his first mission ended in a homicide: the owner of a gas station had resisted the *mara*'s bribery, and, hiring an armed guard, he had constructed an iron fence with wheels to help him shut the station every night. The guard stayed in a hut that doubled as a convenience store that sold popsicles, sodas, and snacks. One night, a *marero* approached the rolling gate and shook it. The noise alerted the guard, who carefully approached to investigate the noise. The *marero* screamed, pretending to be drunk; the guard, lowering his defenses, didn't see *al* Hombrecito , who emerged from the shadows and stuck the barrel of his machinegun through the fence. He unleashed his bullets on the guard. As the sun rose, the body of the guard was found with his pistol held tight, but with no possibility of defending himself.

The headquarters of the *mara* was a house on a cobblestone street that started by a small kiosk in the main street and ended at the cemetery gate. This house belonged to a *mojado* that resided up north, so the house was empty for the most part of the year. *La mara* broke the locks and took over the house as their headquarters.

Ana Luisa's body was discovered the next morning, found at the turn of the gorge, naked and face-down with a mouth full of sand. The rest of her body screamed the signs of torture; her left eye, about to come out of its orbit, was the eternally open witness of a brutal punch. Blood coagulated around giant bruises on cheeks and temples; her lips were swollen and torn; her chest showed bite marks; three stabs to the chest and abdomen testified the end of her life. She was repeatedly raped. Death was merciful to Ana Luisa.

Her family and school friends brought her to her grave in a far-off town. Silence was an accomplice to her death; nobody came to investigate what had happened.

The *pandilla* had sixteen members: five at the cemetery and eleven more on a nearby *barrio*. Not one internal quarrel was known of. Ana Luisa had an uncle in the capital, Plutarco, a military man who fought alongside the *gringos* while stationed at Fallujah in Iraq under Polish orders. In a skirmish, his patrol group had lost several men, and Plutarco fought till the end of his ammunition. Unsheathing his pocketknife and hurt in the thigh, he escaped the ambush after hurting an enemy. He took cover in the shadow of night and came back home like a hero; he retired with a lieutenant rank. According to war chronicles, out of all the Latin-American countries, only El Salvador had sent soldiers to fight and die at the side of the *gringos*. From there on out, no one, no one, had the courage to fight the *mamelucos* and their bullets when they invaded a small neighboring country to annex and steal its petroleum wealth. Plutarco lived with his family in a mid-class neighborhood and was a man of few words; the confidence of one who had triumphed over death erupted out of his eyes.

Plutarco attended his niece's funeral and remained in silence all throughout. He asked no questions before returning to the capital after saying goodbye to his sister and brother-in-law. He had several friends spread throughout sections of the National Security Department; *su compadre* was the present Chief of Police of the neighboring district. Plutarco talked to several old military friends and then to others, the latter recommended by the former.

Five months passed since Ana Luisa's death. On a certain midday a Toyota pick-up arrived into town with three men. After passing the cemetery, the truck parked on the main street beside a kiosk, two blocks from the corner made by the street that runs in front of the cemetery and ends at the main street. Two men jumped out of the truck and made their way up the small cobblestone street that goes from the kiosk towards the cemetery. Before reaching the mareros' house, they stopped at a convenience store to buy Coca Cola and potato chips. They drank their sodas on the front of the store, taking a mental picture of the vacant lots and all the houses from there to the cemetery. Then, they spotted the mareros exiting their stolen house; one of them had a serpent tattoo on the right side of his neck.

The two men concealed their presence with laughter, looking at the opposite side of the road and the mareros, who had already started to walk towards the cemetery. The two men waited a sensible number of minutes at the store and then followed casually towards the cemetery gate. At the entrance, on a cement bench, was El Hombrecito, seated below a sign that read: <WATCH, LISTEN, SHUT UP>. His machine gun rested on his lap. The two men waved at him without entering the cemetery. Instead, they continued on, turning the corner to the right and walking down the street until they hit the main road. They crossed it and continued left, towards the end of town. After two blocks, they stopped under one of the many trees that formed the *Alameda* on the entrance of town. Under the shadow, one of them rested his foot on the thick column that sustained a big cement ball, a solemn reminder of the past. There, they waited for the third man to pick them up and disappeared in the afternoon.

Five weeks later, at 2 a.m., two cars entered town with the silence of the night. Inside them were seven men, masked and set on a mission. They parked near the kiosk and went up the cobblestone street in the direction of the *mareros'* house; they carried two cement battering rams and heavy weaponry of a thick caliber. They silently opened the steel door—no locks—and went up the five or six cement stairs, which led to a cement porch and the main door of the house. Three men surrounded the house up to the patio and the back door and waited for the signal. At the signal, two battering rams broke the front and back doors at the same time. The seven men irrupted into the house.

Their screams woke the *mareros* up as they, guessing what was going on, shouted terrified screams back at them. The mareros put their hands up, surrendering and begging: "Sorry!", "Sorry!", "Please don't shoot."

The machine guns of all seven masked men roared, and the sound was ominous as the bullets ripped through the soft pulp of the bodies, carrying the message of death.

Lico, El Tuco, tried to escape through his bedroom window before he was brought down by sixteen bullets to the core and two to the head. *El marero* with the serpent tattoo cried and begged as the coward he had been all of his brief life before ten bullets destroyed his face.

El Hombrecito de la Metralla was brought down under the small dining room table. A picture of immense terror was over his face: the face of the one who does not know why his life was escaping from him.

Two mareros were left with the opportunity to raise their weapons and fight, but the surprise assault proved to be too much for them. They died holding their guns, riddled by dozens of shots.

Before the hollow silence closed over the ominous house, a war cry against criminals was heard from a masked man: "¡Así te quería agarrar!"

The neighbors were woken up by the shooting and dared not come out of their houses till morning peaked. No one wanted to go inside the house even though the door was left open. And so, the days went on, till a group of young men, probably *pandilleros* from another town, came to town in their old truck and took the corpses of five young *mareros* to be buried off somewhere. At that time, there was no questioning.

The identity of the masked men who avenged the martyrdom of Ana Luisa was never known. Three more months passed, and before the patronal festivities, on a rainy Friday, at 2 a.m., five cars with sixteen masked men drove to four houses, from where eleven *mareros* operated. Their mission was clear. This time around, three of the masked men were injured with bullets; eleven *mareros* died. Only time knew their names, and the memories of the people were sure to bury them.

The Light

It had been a long time since The Light arrived in town. Its first sighting was something of a surprise, for the shining was only possible to see at the highest point of a hill on moonless nights. The hill was a crater left by some sleeping volcano. It took a climb of a thousand meters to get to its top, starting from the intersection at Calle del Calvario: left was the trail that led to the *pilas,* where clothes were washed since the beginning of times; right was Marie Pilar bridge, which crossed the ravine, dividing the town into two parts.

Nobody knows the meaning of the bridge's name, but it is now known by the townsfolk by another name: María del Pilar. Marie was too difficult to pronounce. It is embellished with a railing carved with two young women's faces molded to the central arch's curve, and from it it takes a thousand-meter walk through el Chagüite slope to get to the river and skirt it. As it descends, the river forms into small waterfalls and pools that have always amused the townsfolk. The closer to the top, the more traces of its nature the old volcano showed, when suddenly, at the turn of the trail, through gypsum and clay and pools of hot water, fumaroles emerged from the volcanic rock.

Nobody, not even the *comadres*, who know all essence, could point to the exact arrival of The Light. There were vague ideas of its beginning; the oldest folk affirmed that it predated the arrival of radio and television. When asked about it, they would say: "*Uuuuy*, the shining is older than the times of President Manuel Enrique. According to my mama, one night Manuel Enrique climbed *el* Chagüite to see The Light up-close. When he came back, he launched himself as candidate for the nation's presidency."

Its fame spilled from town all the way to the capital, and there came a day when a group of soldiers, lead by *Teniente Coronel* Chebo Monterrosa, arrived in town. According to common law, having a *teniente coronel* position meant that he had the qualifications to organize a *coup d'état* and take the nation's presidency.

Monterrosa couldn't hide his most intimate desire even as he enrolled himself as a soldier in the army. He was from the West, born to a poor family in a poor town. He was pressed by ambition and wanted to achieve success sooner rather than later. He enrolled in night school and finished with honors. At barely thirty-seven years of age, he got the *teniente coronel* position. Ever since, his curiosity was only occupied by *el* Diccionario de la Real Academia Española, from which he continuously memorized new words to expand his vocabulary, for—as he saw it—a president should embody the epitome of cultural refinement. As he talked to his troop, he tried to sound like an archbishop. His troop was awed and therefore maintained order.

When he got to town, he rounded his soldiers up in the town's central park, paying respect to no one by announcing his arrival, not even to the mayor or the National Guard corporal. As he saw it, those people were already, or would soon be, under his orders.

Monterrosa talked to his army, letting them know their goals for the town: "Our mission in this land is essential, and it's concerned with an unexpected finding, as our duty entails the unveiling of the mystery of this incident. Making contact with The Light will provide its favored with the virtues of a leader."

Soldiers clapped and nodded in approval as he honored them with the widest of smiles. As he headed to be welcomed by the mayor, the soldiers quickly approached one of their own, Tulio Gavidia, who had finished primary school and knew how to read. He could certainly answer their questions. "*Mirá*, Tulio, what does it mean to 'entail'? And what exactly is an 'unveiling'?"

Tulio answered as best he could: "'Entail' is when a dog finally catches its tail, and you know how long *el Teniente Coronel* has been after The Light. As for 'unveiling,' I hear that's what the *cachimbona* fruit is called in Africa. *Onbeili*."

That explanation satisfied the soldiers, so they got ready to climb the hill. For such a requirement, Monterrosa had prepared *yute* sacks smeared with tar on the inside. He had gotten to the following conclusion: "Tar will prevent The

Light escaping through the holes between the *yute* fibers in our sacks." The sacks had a wide mouth that could be closed with a *manta* waistband tied to a cinch rack of the same material, through which a *yute* string ran in order to catch big chunks of Light and rapidly close the sack with no opportunity for The Light to escape. According to Monterrosa, The Light could be slowly taken out of the sacks in order to be given to those who had his favor once he was president. Each soldier had to carry two or three sacks, open them as soon as they got to The Light, and trap as much shining as they could.

They arrived on a rainy, dark, and windy day alongside news of overflowed rivers and flooded regions all through the valley and the coast. Whenever they were asked to postpone their climb in the face of the storm, they would murmur a disengaged, "We're in a hurry."

They were on the bridge at about five o'clock, ready to start the climb towards the crater, and they were already soaked; their sacks weighted more that they should. Yet, obediently, they slowly began the walk as the rain worsened, but as they walked, more problems arose. The full river was about to flood and was too grown on the borders used to climb el Chagüite. Their boots, full to the brim with water, were also muddy with clay, so walking turned harder at every step. In spite of this, the troop was set on reaching the top and filling the sacks with bunches of The Light, for this—they were sure—would make them better people. About a hundred steps before de fumaroles, the full fury of the storm poured on them. The bellow of the wind was deafening, and trees folded and lost branches before its force. One of the branches found the head of a soldier and tackled him with no respect for his helmet. And so, the terror filled the soldiers' moods.

Monterrosa found his mission to be senseless as he told himself, "How could even a quarter of this Light be trapped amidst this wind?" Even as the night was closing in, the troop began its descent. It was every bit as hard as the climb; the paths were treacherous and slippery, and two soldiers fell into one of the pools. Only one made it, as he used his sack to float. The wounded soldier had to be helped down; two of his partners were map and staff to him.

They arrived at the park at midnight. There was no one on the streets. The storm, slightly softened by the surrounding mountains, poured all its impotence on giant streams of rain that became small, fast, furious rivers as they rushed through the cobblestone of the steep streets. The soldiers began getting their food rations out, and surrounded by silence, they ate at the kiosk. Monterrosa gave order to head towards the capital, paying no attention to the wind or the dangers on the road. They all got on their military vehicles and left as they arrived: at night, lost in darkness.

The town never knew what happened to the *Teniente Coronel*, only that there was a failed *coup d'état* stopped by a unit that still was loyal to the president. Monterrosa became a prisoner in his own town until a friend of his gained

31

power, became the new president, and gave him amnesty so that he could retire with his family in the capital.

The town knew then that The Light had to be approached without violence or ambition, with a clean mind ready to learn from it. So, a series of pilgrimages started marching towards the top of the crater. These were in charge of the townsfolk as chapters or fraternities and contributions were welcomed as to offer process to gain the favor of The Light. Yet the most clever, mischievous, abusive ones kept the contributions. All sorts of candidates for municipalities, deputies, and governorships climbed just to reach The Light.

Once, Paco Luna's friends, *mareros*, convinced him to go up the ravine. They had the clear intention of stealing a shred of Light and offering it, at a fair price, to other town rascals. Paco was fresh out of jail for stealing a bicycle, and his friends made him think that once he saw The Light, his life of crime would turn. So, Paco humored them and got as far as a little waterfall that ended in a decent-sized pool. There, he pronounced the following words with a sense of finality: "I won't take another step. I need no Light; I'm clever, *cachimbón*. You go then, I'll go back to town when I feel like it."

The Church also got involved with The Light when they understood it was a pivotal point in the town's life. They feared it might get in the way of or even contradict religious disposition. But luckily, a Spanish priest arrived in town just in time. Clever and well-educated, he explained in his first sermon,

"I have a limited understanding of The Light, and yet I'm sure it stands by my Faith's doctrine." And just like that, The Light and its mystery grew even more profound or even more superficial—depending on the conversation's approach.

All sorts of academics turned their eyes to The Light: professors, philosophers, chemists, occultists, meteorologists. Each one of them had an explanation, which ended in the foundation of the National Light Studies Commission. Books full of scribbles and theories regarding the origin were published, but not one of the academics dared climb the crater. Perhaps they feared the night and its spirits when illuminated by The Light.

As years went by, the town grew accustomed to contemplation of The Light, which maybe also grew out of the necessity for it. That is, until *el Conflicto* exploded with the eloquence of a thousand trumpets. Civil War came with its expected and insatiable death toll. Seventy-five thousand fell; two-hundred-and-sixty thousand were affected: widows, orphans, wounded…the town wasn't untouched by the shadows. It even got to experience the theater of war, the shootings, in its very center. When the shootings ended, corpses piled up, counted and riddled with bullets beside the central park's flower beds. Someone probably wrote a poem about that sight, reveling in the peaking nature of the race, Maya Lenka, which established itself in the skirts of the town's mountain in the beginning of times. That poem might still be framed in the town hall.

War lasted for twelve years. Economical disaster was profound, even for a stoic town that knew poverty well. Exodus towards the North was a necessity, as some families lost it all in *el Conflicto*. This Exodus, composed of thousands of orphaned children, one day would result in a block of *maras* and *pandillas,* with its respective violence, the outrage against innocence, the rapes, the threats, the bribes, the murder of some young relative, some worker, anyone who would stand against them.

A North American president deported a thousand of these young ones; they knew only evil and selfishness,they had no spirit of renovation, no stutter when ending a life; they were revenge experts living off of somebody else's work. This president's name could be read all around the capital—that is, until a new rising government with no sympathy for the gift of a thousand *pandilleros* tore off all signs that read the name of the donor. They threw his name in the trash—"Its rightful place," as the rising government unequivocally said.

That's when The Light's shine was even brighter. "There's something happening," the town's elderly said. "Hopefully something good," replied the *comadres*, and they always know more than what they're saying.

One day, as any other, a Sunday, there came the roaring of the land. Witnesses said the sound was as if big chunks of mountain fell into a deep, invisible lake. The splashing was deafening, and people swore they wouldn't make it out alive. The earthquake lasted for nine full minutes, and it ravaged every single house in town. The colonial church with its bell tower, the pride of the town, broke in pieces in the thin air; the great bell flew and fell on the primary school teacher. A court clerk, as his most crucial moment approached, crumbled over his seat and fell into the septic tank as the ground tore and the tank was exposed by the violence of the earthquake. The fall saved his life, and afterwards he joked that he would never be mad at any mockery about the smelly circumstance, as it was also fortunate.

Ten thousand people died. A military blockade was set, and it lasted three months, until every last corpse was buried and the wreckage was cleaned. Those days were of irremediable loss, and The Light shone brightly, intensely, something never seen before. International help was quick and effective. As always, *gringos* were the biggest donors; as always, the donation ran right through the state representatives' hands. Reconstruction was slow and painful. Italian and Swedish families, established in town for the riches in coffee farms and the climate, closed their homes forever and were lost to the town's history, though there were some valuable exceptions: four or five Italian families and two or three Swiss families stayed to share the misfortune of their town.

During those ominous days, The Light shone, flaring up the mountain like a torch, as a guiding light, a warm hope that stood over misery.

Six years the reconstruction lasted, led by Peruvian companies which were capable of magnificent things. Houses were constructed with anti-earthquake systems, supported by iron columns and cement blocks; asbestos roofing was installed alongside appropriate drainage; septic tanks were forever closed; infrastructure for clean water and electric light promised the town a much more prosperous future. But mistakes were also made: the old, straight streets were lost forever, replaced by an ever-lasting curve that ended nowhere. The central park, ideal for ceremonies, a place for young folk to meet, to break confetti eggs on the head of a beautiful girl, to enjoy Easter, to skate through on placid afternoons over the geometric ceramic tiles (an heirloom left by Manuel Enrique). The central park was utterly demolished. The glazed tiles were replaced by a thick layer of cement; the kiosk where once the *Banda Municipal* played on weekends, stretching and lighting the afternoon, was taken down, replaced by some-thing inaccessible; entrances became exits; there was no good explanation for any of it. Townsfolk, thankful for reconstruction, said nothing and stood resigned to the changes in their old and beautiful town.

Years later, after the earthquake, after the Civil War, there came the invasion of the *pandillas or maras,* and the cultural atmosphere of the whole nation changed. Ideas and words never before heard were added to the juvenile slang—"*La droga*," "*la mara*," all said with an innocent childishness with no regard for the virtue they were betting for: life or death. The elderly were constantly treated without respect; television showed images of young *pandilleros* beating old men out in the streets of our capital city—a ritual for the welcome of new blood to a *pandilla*. Homicides were hard to count. Going out at night was a reckless deed, no matter the town or city. Criminals had more rights than their victims, and frustration gnawed on the nation's soul.

There was no end in sight, and the people felt abandoned. All presidents were unscrupulous, false, awful, dishonest thieves. Don Gustavo Padilla, the town's wise old man, kept saying, "There's nothing viler, criminal, evil, than stealing from poor people." And yet there they were, same ones as always, arrogant as ever, cleverly evil, experts on excuses and full of empty promises. Some of them, even after drying out the public treasury, purchased another nationality and avoided any further persecution, keeping a last piece of "honor." One of them, before leaving the country, had let out the essence of his soul when asked about his thefts: "These foolish people deserve nothing, *hombre*. If I wanted to, I have enough dough to buy the presidency once again."

In town, The Light remained. Instead of giving any sign of dullness, its radiance was more obvious than ever, illuminating the crater like a small sun. People smiled as they saw it, knowing they had a miracle upon their bosom, something reserved for the courageous amidst misfortune; for heroes conquering life; for philosophers and poets who are the diviners of the universe with the mission to expand men's horizons. The possibility of a commotion was latent—maybe even a protest, a social storm which could reframe the course to sustain hope in the history of a town accustomed to suffering, to hunger, to dead ends.

The Light remained, its splendor sometimes altered according to the national sentiment; always beautiful, a sister to joy, exploding on ominous days, residing on happy ones. It had no name. According to its people, it needed none; everybody knew it already. It needed no guarding, either, no fences or walls; anyone who carried a noble face could approach surrounded by the night. If they were lucky, they would make it down the crater with a better understanding of the value of man. Awed, every mind that had once sought an explanation to this wonderful phenomenon, never knew to find humbleness when it is given by wisdom.

And what once was anticipated finally came: that which was required to start a discussion between free people. No more tyranny, no more theft, no more corruption to justice, no more fear in walking the streets in the middle of the night, no more hungry children in schools, only new, respectful learning to seek the broad horizon that would fill their days with joy, taking them to a surprise caused by sudden change; inside them was the only truthful answer.

No more arrogance, insult, or boldness for the country that saw them born.

The Light remained, unchangeable. No one had a guess as to the meaning of that manifestation that had illuminated the minds of the most honest; since the beginning of the nation, two hundred years ago. Its presence was palpable in friendly dealings or bellicose arguments of our people. Those who keep some faith will say, even if they don't fully understand what they are saying, that it will always be this way. The secret will be guarded in the mind of the few, even as the many aspire to be one of them.

All Through the Night

A caravan heading north was being organized at San Pedro Sula's central park. A hundred people kept adding to the eagerness as carpenters, constructors, servers, taxi drivers, and uncountable other adventurers and delinquents joined the commotion. The news had gotten to Tela and even its suburbs.

Chabela Chicas Ibañez lived in the *arrabal de la Charca* with her daughter, Rosa Elvira Chicas Ibañez "La Murci," *la murciélga*, the bat. Rosa was ten years old, chubby, and sunken-faced, with harsh hair that couldn't be braided. She had an easy laugh and a nimbleness about her. Strong and joyous, with her eternally disheveled hair, she was always the first one to be chosen to play *La Chuspa* or *El Ladrón Librado*. She had a weakness for cherries, bat's favorite fruit, hence the nickname. She could be seen with her *guacál de morro* full of the fruit as she climbed any cherry tree that she could lay eyes on, pulled a handful of fruit, and satisfied her feisty palate. Kids at school befriended her just to have themselves a couple of cherries.

Her father, Chepe Ibáñez "Tasajo," was an irresponsible mulatto who left when she was barely six months old; he was a businessman for the *hampa*. He could be seen wandering through every filthy hotel in Tela with a fast pace, offering hosts his product—"Cocaine? Marijuana? Cocaine? Marijuana?"—and then trotting away when his offer wasn't well-received. He knew danger and sadness, as he had spent half his life in prison, detained in gaols at Tela or San Pedro Sula.

On the other hand, Chabela was untiring in her job as a hotel maid in one of the worst establishments in Tela. Her uncle, Rufino Chicas, was the owner. He gave her the job so she could sustain herself and her little daughter at the face of Tasajo's abandonment. This was about ten years ago.

The hotel had access to the sea, touched by an almost unwalkable beach full of trash, vultures, and vermin. It reeked of decomposition. It was more of a shack than a hotel, servicing criminals, drunks, and whores. Its bathrooms had never been thoroughly cleaned. The pillows, bedsheets, and actual beds were never a match, smeared with yellowish stains left by bleach and beach sweat. Poverty was visible on every sheet, on the faded patterns where Donald Duck, Superman, Porky, and Bugs Bunny and friends could be barely guessed at. Rufino had no intention of investing on banishing the filth, and Chabela was the one to suffer it. Filth seemed to be the main and only component of every surface, supporting the very center of each wall.

Chabela, sustained on the minimum wage, scrubbed and scrubbed and scrubbed everything away and then walked back home, aching and tired. Yet the decision to join the caravan was a sudden one. As she walked back home one night, she found a man going over the whole of his house with the intention of finding a way in. Rosa Elvira was inside, alone, doing homework as always. Chabela shrieked at the intruder, alerting the neighbors. The *hampón* left, lost in the thickness of the bushes. That night, fighting with the sudden consciousness of her abandonment and misery, she sat beside her daughter and declared, "We have to get away from here."

After ten years of slaving work, Chabela had saved about five thousand dollars. She began with the preparations for the trip. Inside her head, a place briming with hope, honor, and respect was awaiting her as a just compensation for a life of hunger, honorable work, and sacrifice. She began by collecting little bars of soap, mostly used, left by the hotel hosts. Rufino was final with his decision to lend her no money, not even as a reward for the years of service. In the ten years she had worked for him, her wage was never raised. So, she bought two second-hand backpacks and a *manta* bag. La Murci prepared her own bag, a colorful stringed *matata* bought at the *Feria de Tela*. The final arrangements were made throughout several days, under the hanging fear of forgetting something crucial. They choose sets of clothes for warm and cold weather and avoided packing heavy things, as they anticipated a long walk. Rosa carried jerky and smoked meat, dry cheese, *chengas*, water, and cherries. The departure was set for August, so they would get to the frontier in September, avoiding the Texan summer heat, which had killed many.

Chabela had a cousin who lived in North Carolina and worked at the city, in a furniture factory. The city used to be prosperous, and it even had prestige in the furniture business. The industry was composed of more than ten factories, but these began to close in order to be moved to an eastern country. Labor and transportation was cheaper in that country, plus there was no need to pay taxes, and importation prices were nonexistent when furniture reentered the United States. Greed has no price, but in the city, an unbearable wave of unemployment caused the flight of most of its people. Some factories remained, doing the impossible to keep their employees and avoiding bankruptcy.

It was Chabela's dream to work for one of those factories. She imagined herself learning tapestry, being congratulated by the owners for being the best at it. Whenever she felt sad, that thought brought a smile to her lips. "Chabela doesn't fear work," "Chabela will thrive; her daughter will have a godly education," she told herself. This virtuous dream gave her the spirit to endure life's offenses. "I'm almost there," she said, almost praying. "I'm almost there," echoed her soul.

La Murci said goodbye to her friends and to her teacher, Doña Marina Cienfuegos, who was tall, thin, and proud, as anyone who knows their own value is. She was beautiful in her youth, white, with elongated eyes; everyone at school was in love with her. She always wore blue, and that's how she was drown by her admirers; *Niña Marina*, read the drawings. Loved by all, patient before dullness, rough with the mischievous, unyielding when punishing bullies. She rejected a position as school principal, for teaching was her passion. Love, patience, civic mindedness for her adored homeland: she wanted to get all these inside kids' heads by force of pure repetition. "He who knows more can do more."

La Murci gave her a tender hug, tears spilling from her eyes. Doña Marina hugged her back, knowing she wouldn't ever see her again.

The caravan, carrying its two thousand souls, started walking towards the south. They entered Guatemala through the Copán frontier on a winter afternoon, accompanied by rain that was impertinent in its lightness. Yet the caravan was grateful for it; it freshened them, inciting them to hurry their steps. *Conqué* had to be eaten fast on the brief opportunities for rest while enduring an atmosphere filled with the howls of children. Rolled in aluminum paper, as was the rest of their food, *chengas* were split in half: half for La Murci, half for Chabela. They had to last, along with the cheese and the meat, as long as possible, long enough to face strange wastelands, strange people. But as for now, they felt embraced by the multitude, safe; there was no lack of opportunity to form friendships, to promise mutual help in case of any difficulty.

And so, the night of their arrival in Copán came and went with no fuss. The morning was fresh and bright. Optimism, hope, and an eagerness to get there made early risers out of everyone. They were camped on Copán's surrounding lands, but the people who led the caravan were already seeing the guarding posts in Guatemala's frontier. They had to wait for employees to arrive so the process to cross would be set into motion and they could continue with their march. As the sun fully rose, the caravan was past the frontier, and so were Chabela and Rosa. Rickety buses and pick-up trucks offered transportation to Jalapa-Sanarate at a fair price, so Chabela and Rosa paid. They got into the back of a truck alongside twenty-six other people who also found the price fair. Packed like sardines, they headed downtown.

"Excuse me. Excuse me," Chabela said as she made her way through the mass. The pick-up was specially prepared with a welded metallic fence on its sides to fit the most people, though everyone was standing as Chabela secured a place in a corner of the fence and with her back against the cabin of the truck. She crossed her hands over the shoulders of her daughter in a protective attitude. As uncomfortable as it might have been, it saved them a hundred kilometers on foot.

Arriving at Sanarate, another hundred people were already waiting for the rest of the caravan. They had already made arrangements for transportation to Guatemala's border with Mexico. This trip took another five hours, and it stopped at the capital for a change of bus. Then, it took them to La Mesilla.

They ate from their own rations on the bus, then bought a roasted chicken with tortillas for dinner. When they finally got to La Mesilla at midnight they were exhausted and stiff from the cold. They took refuge at the porch of a closed store. Backpacks were pillows; *chumpas* were sheets.

The night was full of omens. As rumor ran, Mexican *coyotes* were harsh and abusive; they asked for impossible sums plus the favor of carrying drugs all trough Texas. In exchange, they offered security through Eagle Pass, which avoided the Río Grande. Anguish took over them: they laid awake, unable to rest.

The pact between *coyotes* and border employees was obvious. The latter let immigrants through; the former charged for passage to Mexico. So, inside the caravan, alliances formed, too, some based on region, nationality, and so on. Promises were made: they wouldn't part ways until they arrived in Texas. They made up signals that meant help, danger, and agreed-upon other useful things. Though the caravan had its origin in San Pedro Sula, a hundred other immigrants had joined them along the way. No doubt more people would join them as they passed through Mexico.

The sun rose at La Mesilla. Touched by the sun, the fertile tropic, bright with August rains, peacocked its colors as an endearing smell rose, healing the soul. It was sad for those who were soon to leave that paradise.

Passage through Mexico's border was hard and humid, and the heat had started to rise since ten in the morning. At midday, Chabela and La Murci were showing their papers at the migration counter and then crossed a hall with its walls bursting with pictures of all the wonders of the country.

Mexico is one of the most beautiful countries in the world, yet it harbors cruel men, criminals incapable of hearing the howls of their victims. These men know no reason when faced with a dilemma; they know no rest once the chase for their neighbor's money begins; they would never stop at something so small as law, or peace, or people. Interference of their machinations is charged with the death of their enemies; their ranks are full of *sicarios* that will enjoy ending their victim's life. As they say, "*Un tiro en la cabeza, no le fallo.*"

They came to a little patio at the end of the hall. There was barely the necessary in it: a washbasin for refreshment and some filthy outhouses. Chabela remembered the hotel in Tela. The patio was full of migrants conversing with Mexicans who were probably *coyotes*, as Chabela judged from their mannerisms. One of them approached her, and after questioning her, he proposed a deal: to take her to the Texas border, either by bus or train, for the price of two thousand dollars. Or, for three thousand dollars, to take them to Eagle

Pass, inside Texas. Chabela had promised some companions that they would travel together, so she was in no rush to make a decision just yet. She wanted to wait for her friends so they could decide together, cross together.

At 3 o'clock, all the friends met on the patio. They decided to board two pick-ups that would take them to Tonalá, avoiding the mountains in San Cristobal de las Casas. Each paid a hundred dollars. They were twenty in total, ten in each truck.

There was a palpable rivalry between the drivers. The ones who drove to Tonalá weren't allowed to take passengers to Arriaga; there was an excessive fee for it. So, Tonalá passengers were expected to make the rest of the way on foot. Thirty kilometers took them to Arriaga; one hundred and thirty-five kilometers more took them to Juchitán. From there, they could either make it to Veracruz, then Texas, or reach the center of the country through the Pacific Ocean. The latter would take them to Arizona or Mexicali.

The twenty women were looking to get to the east of the United States. Like Chabela, they had family and friends offering hospitality. They arrived in Tonalá at midnight. Chabela and Rosa ate the leftovers from the roasted chicken, taking shelter in the train station. They needed to rest; the next day promised a lot of walking.

At 5 o'clock in the morning, they were woken up by the arrival of a train. But they had decided not to board La

Bestia; they knew the danger it entailed. It was better to walk and wait for a good Samaritan to give them a ride to the next town than expose themselves to the brutality of strangers. It was raining an enviable storm, like all of those formed in the tropic; enviable for their ire, their stubbornness, lasting days, flooding rivers and towns, destroying crop fields, increasing poverty that was already endless in South America. Storm and all, it was imperative to move.

The twenty women in a caravan of seven hundred people began the trip through a highway in Juchitán. Some parishes had help committees designed to supply water and food to migrants as they crossed through their towns. Some of those migrants, instead of thanking the help from noble Mexicans, complained about the small rations of bread, eggs, beans, and salsa. It was a joke that got what it deserved, for someday the committees would dissolve, and there would be no more awnings on the side of the road, with Mexicans in those awnings offering water, bread, and something to eat to the migrants; Mexicans as poor as the migrants but carrying in their souls the "noblesse that oblige," the one that persists in the foundations of nations that inherited greatness since their beginnings, and it followed them in their walk over this earth.

With no further complications, the caravan made it to Piedras Negras. There, they would be witnesses to the most ominous spectacle known to humankind. *Coyotes* at Piedras Negras were a part of an organization of drug dealers that distributed their product in most cities and towns of

Mexico and the United States. Their influence was massive, and they were responsible for the deaths of three hundred people per day. This is only counting overdoses; deaths from gun violence were another story.

The twenty women arrived at Piedras Negras. It was Friday, and the air was hot. They felt some beastly eyes follow their steps closely, discreetly, as they settled in a small hotel. Everything about them was already known by the cartel leaders, informed by *coyotes*. The leaders were known for their cruelty and anonymity, and they were covered by shadows, directing their ranks from there. They need not show their faces to collect their multimillionaire benefits provided by bribery, drug distribution, and the boom produced by the arrival of uncountable immigrants that wandered the streets and clustered around borders, hungry for an opportunity to get through.

Out of all the henchmen, the protagonist was Rafael Garza Gaytán "El Beibi," the baby. He had symmetrical features, handsome; women were fond of his company, his money. He had a gun buddy, Rafael Vaquerano "El Gringo"; forty years old, green eyes, tall, muscular, dressed in *botas y sombrero*, like a Texan. Formerly, he had been a schoolteacher on a little town east of Coahuila, but he was seduced by the lucrative drug trafficking. Of that cartel, three were the favorite sicarios: Tomás Apodaca "El grillo," with a queue of a dozen dead bodies, skinny, petite, a scar on his left cheek, the product of a prison quarrel; Juan Ramón Acuña "El Mickey," with sharp features and a profuse jaw, he wore a small mustache that was more like moss and made him look like a mouse; Joaquín Hernán Garza Garza "El Charro," El Beibi's cousin, who was an almost two-meter-tall giant, slender and strong, a great drinker and unyielding criminal. The cartel had connections on Eagle Pass: Mexicans who received illegal products and distributed them in the country.

Some of the border agents, Texans, were colluded with the *cartel*, and either their absence or presence was controlled by their orders. Michael Ray Villaseñor patrolled the deserted roads around the Río Grande. He was clever in a way; he knew how to manipulate the cartel to the point where it was impossible to truly know how involved in their operation he was. How was it that drugs, capable of such death, terrible agents in the life of the young, could reach even small towns of Maine and New Hampshire? Villaseñor was only one of the links in the formidable chain of distribution.

It was 6 o'clock when the *coyotes* burst into the hotel where the twenty women were staying. They were hunting them, ready to approach them and make them a proposition, *pasarlas al otro lado*, where they would be welcomed by an adequate form of transportation that would take them into the country. And they didn't have to wait. They intercepted three women who left their room to get something to eat only three minutes into their surveillance. The *coyotes* greeted them with respect and let them know that, for only three thousand dollars per head, they would take them to the United States. That was too high for the women; after a brief bargaining, it was concluded that they would charge two thousand per adult and one thousand per child.

They would leave at 11 p.m. to avoid the patrols in Texas, which lasted from eight to twelve hours, ending and starting at eleven. The idea was to entirely bypass the bridge that connects Eagle Pass and Piedras Negras and instead travel by rafts from Mexico to Texas, where a bus would be waiting to take them north.

The women were excited. They gathered their money and nervously waited for the night. As previously agreed upon, two buses were waiting for them in an alleyway near the hotel. Each one could carry twelve people. In arriving, the women found that two other young Mexicans would be joining them. They looked about twenty-five. One of them had her nose pierced on the left side and two funny-looking tattoos on her left arm. They introduced themselves to the twenty women, telling them that they were looking for a better fortune up north. One of them had family in Chicago that she was going to visit. The other said nothing, only that she was heading to New York. She didn't seem to be very fond of talking. Though they had to squeeze in the buses, they seemed calm. As they exited the city through the right, they saw the bridge that led to Eagle Pass.

They entered Highway 2, on the direction to Ciudad Acuña, which is about ninety kilometers from Piedras

Negras. They drove past a border post with no further questions. Surely there was a sort of understanding between the *coyotes* and the guards. A few kilometers ahead, a sign read "San Carlos," pointing to the exit on the left, which led to a narrow road of gravel and dirt. The women asked why they would turn left if the river was to the right, and they were told that first they had to pick up the rafts to cross the river.

After driving for a few minutes, the buses left behind any sign of a real highway and ventured through a dusty path full of overgrown vegetation, bordered by barbed wire fencing that seemed to continue all through the darkness of night. At the end of the path, the space widened and at fifty meters from there set a rectangular building made of corrugated aluminum. From that angle, the building seemed to have two heights: at the left, it stood six meters high, the entrance to the building consisted of a single wooden door that opened to the inside of the building, as well as a screen door that opened to the outside. At the right, the building stood ten meters high, with ventilation windows on the sides. Four big gates, big enough for trailers to pass through, occupied the front. The main entrance was guarded by three men, El Gringo, El Mickey and El Grillo, whom the women didn't know. Upon seeing them, apprehension took over them. But the *coyotes* reassured them that everything was alright, the stop would be brief, and they could use that time to go to the bathroom while they secured the rafts to the buses. So, they all got out.

As they entered the budling, El Grillo tried to hide his scar. El Beibi y El Charro welcomed them to a small living room with chairs and sofas. Astonished by the El Charro's height, the women grew more nervous, and he tried to calm them down with a few jokes. They were offered water and showed the way to the bathroom, which they all used. After that, all they could do was wait as the five men stood over them in the room, near the doors. At one point, one of them approached them, offering to give all their money back, plus two hundred dollars more, if they only helped them cross some products over the border. By products, they meant a coke brick covered in plastic, and a plastic bag full of rounded, colorful pills that reminded Murci of the mint candy sold at the Tela Fair. Chabela immediately knew what the products were and proceeded to give her reasons not to carry them over the border. She knew that drugs could only lead to misfortune. The living picture was Tasajo, going in and out of prison in the name of business. "I can't expose my daughter this way. What if I end up in prison?" she said. "Please keep the money."

Another woman, Luz Socorro Sánchez Smith "Lucita" offered her apologies, too, stating that she couldn't risk being a mule. Mulatta, beautiful and proud of her figure, she worked in a shoe shop in San Pedro Sula. She was honest and tidy and dreamt of being a nurse, though she abandoned her studies, as poverty needed her full-time attention. Her family consisted of her mom, a seamstress in the town market, and two younger brothers, who lived in a shack in the *tugurios* of San Pedro Sula. She was a Christian and lived with integrity and optimism, which she shared with everyone around. Before leaving, she said goodbye to her friends at the choir. They used to sing every Sunday, happily brightening the services. Her friends cried and kissed her and commended her path to God.

The *narcos* looked at each other. "That's ok," one of them said as the others gave instructions to the other women who had accepted the offer and were changing their own clothes for a white t-shirt that was marked with a certain logo of a certain company. This shirt guaranteed their safe passage. These seventeen women were marched down to the buses. They had made space in their backpacks for the drugs. The two young Mexicans, chatting with two men, boarded a sedan of five passengers. The car disappeared into the night; these women were part of the *cartel*. The bus followed. Carrying the product, they headed towards the river, towards the dream, towards Texas.

Chabela, La Murci, and Lucita remained in the living room with the five men of the Piedras Negras cartel. They were instructed to change their clothes and put on yellow t-shirts. They could already feel the approaching danger. These t-shirts signaled that, even though they had paid for safe passage, they were not carrying drugs. Anything they said would now lead to violence.

El Charro took them into another room that looked like an office. El Grillo followed and sat in one of the chairs after pouring himself a cup of black coffee from a machine in the corner of the room, next to the outhouse in which the women could change their clothes. Lucila was the first in the outhouse. As she emerged with her yellow t-shirt, she was instructed to follow el Grillo, who would take her to the river to show her how to cross. They went out the door that led to the garage; El Beibi y El Gringo were waiting for them. With no explanation, they pushed her to the center of the garage. She felt herself be filled with terror, predicting she was going to be a victim of some heinous act. The men sat her in a chair and tied her up to prevent an escape. Her screams of protest ended as the chloroform entered her lungs, and piously, she lost consciousness. This saved her from the knowledge of the acts the five beasts were about to commit.

They threw her over a mattress that was on the ground next to a table with scissors, tools and packing tape. They undressed her and raped her till she regained consciousness. As they put her clothes back on, they offered her a soda. She rejected it. She knew what had happened, but she remained silent, swallowing her tears. They took her back to the living room, shaking, sobbing, and defeated. She sat on one of the sofas, and with her hands covering her face, she lowered her head over her knees and shed the last tears of helplessness that still remained in her wounded soul. In silence, she awaited her fate.

Back in the office, Chabela and La Murci were thinking of her, trying to guess at what had happened. They remained in silence for nearly an hour, also awaiting their fate. The *narcos* had locked the door behind them. El Mickey reappeared and ordered Chabela to go into the outhouse and put on the yellow shirt. She refused to do it without her daughter, but El Mickey pushed her in and locked the door. He lifted La Murci and took her directly to the mattress. She kicked and bit, and the other four seemed so amused by it that they celebrated with a sardonic laugh. Her kicking revealed her intimacy covered by pink underpants made of cheap nylon, like all the underpants of the poor made of cheap nylon. Her own screams were followed by her mother's. Chabela's horror was such that she passed out in order to not die. As she came back, the building was surrounded by a macabre silence. Night brought to her soul the most fatal omens.

Someone, maybe El Grillo, opened the outhouse door and saw that Chabela had a big bruise on the center of her forehead. She had fallen on the toilet when passing out. Chabela felt weak and anxious; her hope was broken. She asked to see her child. The man assured her that La Murci was okay, but he told her she was taken to the hospital in Ciudad Acuña because, as she tried to escape, she had taken a fall and needed medical attention. He assured Chabela that as soon as La Murci could travel, she would be taken to her, wherever she was. Chabela insisted on seeing her immediately. The man reminded her that it was his duty to take her to Texas. It couldn't be any other way.

At 4 o'clock in the morning, Chabela and Lucita exited the building and got into the sedan. They resisted and were met with violence; they were afraid. They were told they would be driven to the river, where they would find a rope in a bend. The rope would guide them and support them all the way to Texas. The *narcos* had only let them live on behalf of El Gringo, the only one who couldn't bring himself to abuse La Murci. He refused even to see and excused himself, claiming he needed to use the bathroom. Maybe because he had been a teacher in a primary school in a poor and isolated town of Coahuila that he found in the smallest corner of his rotten soul the last piece of goodness left in him and made him to not be a part of such dishonor for such a defenseless child.

On their journey, Lucita and Chabela held each other's hands, and their tears fell as one in a sincere and prolonged embrace; this represented the constant pain of the poor, trampled by the tyrants who always seek to steal from the rest a piece of land, a portion of their belongings, a portion of their life and, finally, all their hope, the last treasure of the poor. Still embraced, they got off the car and walked towards the river, in search of the rope that would protect them until the smooth shores of Texas.

Other immigrants were with them, some dressed in white t-shirts and some in yellow. Chabela and Lucita no longer had backpacks nor money; they were left with some pants, a cap and their t-shirt. And in that simple gesture stood all the *narcos'* cruelty, always looking for immediate pleasure, looking to satisfy their lowest instincts, laughing at their own impunity, the one bought and the one taken.

They all crossed and went up the river's shore, two meters high, and they found a lonely street where there used to be cars waiting. These cars were long gone, occupied by the women who accepted carrying the product. Chabela and Lucita, alone and hopeless, began the walk to San Antonio, always looking, always searching for the border patrol.

The following days were painful. Immigrants had to help them with clothes and money. They found refuge in a San Antonio church, where they were given permission to live in the basement with other immigrants, regaining strength and hope.

Chabela finally made it to North Carolina, to her cousin's house. She helped Chabela get a job in the same factory as her. Chabela prospered; she was tenacious and even got to be a manager. The rest of her life was tied to the possibility of getting news about her daughter. Anything that could lead to the whereabouts of her dear Murci.

Lucita made it to Virginia, where a relative awaited. Her faith helped her through the horrible acts that were made against her. She joined the community of her town, where she was embraced and protected. She got a job at a shoe shop and finished her studies. Eventually, she became a nurse for a hospital in her town, just as she dreamed of. Her life was one of kindness towards her patients as she specialized in the care of people who suffered from cancer.

The Rape Tree

Days had passed since the tragedy of La Murci, when a Texan border patrol followed a turn in the road which led them to a mesquite tree. Hanging from the branches of the mesquite were a ragged pair of pink underpants made of cheap nylon: the remnants of a cruel torture. They had stains of dried-up blood and saliva mixed with black coffee. There it hung, the testimony for outrageous impunity and arrogance.

For the perpetrators, the cries of a little girl and her mother move to nothing more than disdain; tears don't reach them. Tyrants have no piety.

Immigrants, all of them, come from countries where corruption is king. Their thief governors force them out of their homeland in search of a little dream: dignity. Dignity that can be found just around kindness towards everyone else and persistence in honest work, that which lifts their foreheads up high when they walk amongst the princes of the earth.

Book of
the Traveler

The Traveler's Poems

The Traveler

For those in my sweet old homeland
who didn't come to be, who couldn't arrive.

For I have nothing more
than a saddlebag
with no olives even,
old and empty and torn,
to fill it only
with dreams
or perhaps feelings,
important to no one,
interesting to no one
but only to the traveler,
the one I do not know,
the stranger poet,
who carries in his brain
the fertile word
that breaks the uncertainty
and for whom nothing lacks,
not even knowledge.

That stranger, that traveler,
is not of my times and yet
still lingers

in the wind's seasons.
Or perhaps he walks,
face covered,
so no one should know
what is hidden in silence,
what we deserve not,
what our arrogance hasn't
come to own.
It hasn't been my fortune
to meet him, or to hear
the sound of the garments
that breaks with uncertainty,
that fills the saddlebag
in which I can't even fit
a handful of dreams.

(Written in 1987, at night)

Blue

Blue,
engraved blue
on wind's turnings
and the sphere,
water's reflection,
generous spark
that generated life.
Patterned blue
is on the wise one's voice
inherent,
the hero's myth,
the nobleness of a tree,
the laughter of children and the whistle
of the mount birds.
Inclined blue,
you who gathers notes
about men and nobility
for hymns to begin,
a tender hand
for sickness,
kindness for failure,

virtues that touch supreme goodness,
fly of the wing,
laughter of children
and whistle of the mount birds.
Hopeful blue,
a door for exiting
the eternal spin
of the death.
Color blue
from the highest angle
of that noble rumor:
thought.
Dawning blue where dreams
sway with the wind's leaves,
beauty of the tree,
song of the children
and the whistle of the mount birds.

Zontzil[1]

the gentle wind
that shelters words in their blue,
the music of the tree and the numbers;
Zontzil amongst clouds
and tops and mountains
where the poem is born in history
as mankind walks;
the guts of my kind,
the color of birds
and the comings and goings of thought;
Zontzil in hope
and in searching

---

[1] The creative breath of the Lenka (Jaguar People) culture.

Far

For Dr. Alejandro Pozuelo Azuela, a friend and comrade
at UNAM's School of Medicine, just as I hear of his
passing in Costa Rica, his beloved nation.

It stays in place,
the pine;
the wind
a thousand circles wailing;
time shortening
its arrival;
back and forth the tide
as it realizes
that behind
it leaves a broken hope,
an un-wet stone,
when forever departing.

Your Music

Your music
is the feeling of distance never-ending;
my solitude's too crowded without your music.
Your music
is the feeling of distance never-ending,
is the feeling of ending no beginning,
no cease, no limit.
Your music in laughter, voice and cry,
my solitude's too crowded without your music!
My solitude, your music...
Get close in a moonless night,
walk close in a moonlit night,
closely watch time's mirror through so many nights.
My dreaming, your music...
Rises my dreaming to look at you, if that,
and music pours out of the stars,
pours out of any silence:
My dreaming sees you,
touches you
and you've always been far,
always and now more than ever.

Eyes in my dreaming can't reach you
as fingers in my dreaming can't touch you...
Eyes in my dreaming!
fingers in my dreaming!
My solitude's too crowded without your music!

Sunset

Towards sunset all eternal
mirror reaches laughter through your ages,
timidity in flourishing uncertainty
in a day so close to living
so far from dying
that the path towards the sky smiled
towards the sacred instant that saw you born.
Little nightingale,
little river of illusion
that on its way gathers prayers
made of motherly caresses,
of tenderness and playfulness.
Towards sunset all eternal:
you will prevail, no matter
the weight that fate imposes,
the shadow that rips all hope,
the mist as it rises, ready to live
of the light
of the above
of all that is beautiful.

Gravity, Poetry of Solitude

Gravity
as an inspiration blows in the distance,
the hand ready to catch
to confine
to own
and fill
with the words I might say once I have it.
Grave and dry,
known not by the everyday oak
nor the worn-out mountain
nor the permeable obituary that walks
as if hunting
once I approach
where the oak has been injured
and I've learnt to dream,
there where illusion is tumultuous and reaches
but one reasoning
with no intention,
brittlely exiled from myself
and all I've loved,
in this rain eternal.
I'll approach

grave and dry,
dream-maker, fear-maker,
uneasy remnant of life,
requiem for a home,
smoother of timely vertigo;
with no intention
I'll distance myself with you
as I let go,
defeated by silence,
poetry of solitude,
dull horizon at the corner of time,
footing your doorstep
as if watching the oak through a new skin,
grave and dry,
with no intention.

Lonely...

lonely,
at the intimate instant
of knowing you so far,
of feeling you so far,
keeping myself from touching
on behalf of the distance,
I wait here
fearful of your sudden appearance
inside a new skin
with a new voice
but still yours
yet strange to my touch
and my ears
and still yours

Pillar

Even in sorrow,
even in deed,
the grace that's passing
has come to need
the hope of morrows,
the hope to yearn:
So light be gentle;
so light be kind
to keep my candle,
to keep my star:
No wind, no sparrow
would find ajar
my flame unguarded,
my night so far.

Above Reproach

Above reproach, He said;
as the light of the sun,
not through the glass
or the water,
not even through the wind;
but nothing in between
the pure light and the knowing.
Above reproach, He said,
just then and only then
you can deserve the touch
of the truth of the angel.
Just then and only then
you will no longer write
the memory, the alchemy,
the irremediable sense
of changing gold
for lead;
of changing life
for death...
Just then and only then

My People

Land where oblivion
forever hides
inside the old seed
or the new fallen foliage;
where the chirping of the bird
affirms its hope
upon the oldest mountain
that dares mimic its sound;
land where men discuss
with the land so infinite
that dreaming grows
and robes.
From it could only
spring a sadness
that overflows all doors,
where silence prays on
its own origin
upon history-filled pools,
upon rivers full
of their offspring's blood.

Oh the death! called upon
as a tribute to the *hampa*,
through a spit-filled mouth,
a killing laugh.
The plastered palm,
the riddled door,
the juicy park
briming with chunks of our brothers.
No more, says the floating angel,
perched upon his stone,
walking broken streets,
living in closed-shut houses
where fear is lord.
No more, says the boy,
growing below a commotion
that grinds all life
and stops all future with a single blow.
My land, my people!
I've seen you die.
I've seen you die.

Song of the Lenka

[I]
Lord of Lamatepec,
I've lost my fortune there,
and at the edge of Huaycarí,
the greenness of Chinchontepec
I turn my back to see
a jungle just as my reign could be:
Jungle that saw it all lost,
all that I could call mine.

Over the temple of Tepotztli,
I made my enemy bleed,
yet my blood was lost
like a sinking halo
in the plateaus of Tenochtli
where lies the thickened *mají*
from where nothing comes back.

[Chorus]
Lordship of Guazapa,
Lordship of Petén,
more harm is done than good
the old squash that rigs,
the Lenka from the hills of Chinameca and Jucuapa.

[II]

I am not at all sincere,
I always carry a machete,
and a nuisance are the ages,
as I gaze at the morning star
that lights the roads
of uncertain and eternal,
a *zenzontle* will interrupt
the pride of the strong,
and the song of the dead.

I have been yesterday's legend,
and the most beloved tribe,
and in the corners of my being
or in the shadow of the signal
I carry the price of life.
I shred and hurt
or make a path out of
the pain that hides,
I'm a Lenka from the hills
from Chinameca and Jucuapa.

[III]

I'm no more than a carcass
who made a Khali from the wind,
and life waits for me,
on the fireplace,
I feel the murky stubbornness
that persists in luck
and pushes me towards the truth

of a face-to-face encounter
with that which I've never been;
I'm walking across this world
with a name that is not mine;
not a warrior of one color,
not a serpent of this hill:
from horizon to horizon,
there's no story if there's no feat,
and all across this map
I'm a Lenka of the hills
from Chinameca and Jucuapa.

[Chorus]
I covered the earth in green,
in dreams the field,
in richness the gut
that I reached for that first time;
I covered in a century the step:
I'm a Lenka of the hills
from Chinameca and Jucuapa.

[IV]
You won't see me there again,
In the dance of the *guarumo*,
In the pirouettes of the smoke
that resemble my parting;
oh, yesterday's slack,
oh, you master of the infinite,
that in your kindness the return

shall arrive piece by piece
with no more fortune than faith
from what now surrounds me
in this sadness scarce:
What I remember it was
the patrimony of my line
and inheritance of old age.
In this road you see
my only cry that wills
that which is solitude,
and the brightness that unveils
the shriek of my truth,
or at the edge of the stinger
of the scorpion's fury:
I'm a Lenka of the hill
from Chinameca and Jucuapa.

[Chorus]
Lordship of Guazapa,
Lordship of Petén,
more harm is done than good
the old squash that rigs
the Lenka from the hills
of Chinameca and Jucuapa.

Barcelona Cries, Cries for the Dead Ones

August 17, 2017, after the criminal charge against
Bercelona's La Rambla, which welcomed them with
affection as they came to Spain all ragged and hungry.

Coldness black entraps
the town with ice,
in the shadows of uncertainty,
in that which I once had,
and dresses me in grief
I still remember.
Solitude in infinite sank,
dream smoke,
rubble imagined
in a word never spoken;
trinkets owned by hatred
that simultaneously spill the secret:
hope,
come back.

I must remain
in spite of the light detached from your eyes,
tear-softened canvas.
I must remain here,
filling the void
as to deceive hate,
or love,
or vice,
and I will burry my nails in this old ground,
it will be my escort as you pass me by,
and I will silently wait,
honoring the night till your return.
Your absence is present,
never-ending pain
gnawing away, hurting
its way to the top,
the only place where
the turning point is reached,
the point where
all audacity ends
and there lies the secret
for that clinging fog
that leads to oblivion.
For having lost you
I lost life,
but never did I lose your absence,
but never did I forget to look at you:

Clinging desire,
all love lost,
all far-off longing
that peaks the instant,
in the hour distant
where remembrance is;

since now I have
to mend my dreaming,
and surrender to the persistence
of never looking back at you,
and so carrying hope
till the turning point
where that fog begins
to lead to oblivion.

For Mexico

For Mexico, in the testing hour, after
the carnage of September 19, 2017.

As field,
as foundation,
as a road for my step
I have only the light of the universe.
I am brightened
by the dream allegory
which devours tragedy;
I entrust life
to its own mystery.
I am faithful to life only,
since that first log
that shapes my longing
till a last breath
dragging the foliage.
I am since the beginning,
since blood's first heartbeat,
till the heroes' last yell,

those heroes who tear
with sharp nails the cliffs
and open a crack in the rubble,
and over their own shoulders carry
tons of hope and soil,
nailing their light to shadow,
weighing life,
defeating death.
My children turned to silent heroes;
I am the immortal land because of them,
I know their names,
their hidden spirit,
the mysterious force
that cuts the call to nothingness.
For me, no more ashes,
no more glowing embers.
I predate my very presence;
mine are the omens
and my steps follow me
towards eternal truth covering.
I am what's to come,
the fight where dying is defeated,
and dying ends.
Mexicans I teach
to overcome tragedy,
raise walls
that cut off the horizon.

One step behind fate,
I order its direction,
the sing that bothers me
with the lifting of tenderness
for those who miss it,
for those I lost
and keep inside my silence
above the immortal rock of my foundation.

Lest You Forget

For Mexico. For Barcelona.

When nothing remains:
The shadow of a shadow,
the last sound
of what used to be voice,
the light in your eyes,
the endless night
that the fibers buried
and chased away life,
the omen of an age alike
approaching,
steep by the echo
where memory starts:
A longing so eager to stay in time
forever, forever…
There, defeated, I'll be
in the first corner you search for,
there where you know
I was hurricane
in tears that sieged my eyes,
that sieged my eyes.
Offspring that sprouted

from that old earthquake
of solitude born in the gut
amidst tenderness,
a fled breath
in search of silence,
there in the last of all goodbyes,
the fury conquered
by the infinite pain
of seeing you no more.
There, I'll be with you,
in each name written
for a requiem
to go alongside your story,
towards the wide horizon
gashed, ended;
your step interrupted
by a strange hand
that since was coming,
there where shadow is born,
where shadow is born.
Follow my step,
breath elevating my lost
and restless hope,
haste

that I crouch on my blood.
I cut off the future
so it remains, looking
through its fingers
for the signal hidden,

a shyness of being
the best of your parts,
carried on embers,
on pieces of the soul
I buried with you
lest you forget.
Lest you forget.

Since Then

Let it not cut the step
or the search of that alchemy
that turns the treasure
of war-used heil into the high hatred
of brother against brother.
Let it not cut the step,
that old longing that presses on my bones
since forever, from afar:
The virtue of following
the very breath of my wind,
the boil of my blood
or even the settled calm of my memory.
Learnt from me only to renew life,
turn it into the image
upon the mirror,
to raise life and mat ready to lunge,
that which embellishes my boot's pompoms,
which has been and always will be,
which I drive across,
galloping towards that final
refuge of fate,
mine, my own,
where I prune my children,

those that have been,
those that watch me with winking eyes
if so to better understand the passage of time
and the liquid fear of my frontiers
that hope not to
be cut off in the step,
true alchemy
that turns ideas
and horizons,
that turns into straw
those rocky walls
that cut off the step
of the crest of my unease,
those that press on my bones
and push out the scream
I've carried since forever,
at the foot of fortune,
at the shadow of fate
that I dare look for
and turn
in the name of my children,
those I nail to my mind
ever since I'm history,
ever since old glory,

lineage and seed,
the coin that wedges in
the definite profile,
mi name is Cataluña,
judge of my longing,

voice in the path,
pompon for my boot
that which I drive in the step,
guidance stuck,
in that old life-defining duty.

Ukraine

A Good Reason

Paths were made
to be followed;
farse and slogan,
ways to hold
a weapon:
lies.
We were all happy
till the day man asked:
What am I doing?
Why do I feel lonely?
Could I speak differently?
Then on an evening as any other
several gathered
in an unlikely scream, just asking
to watch the sun from another window.
Then came the circus,
a farse tank-defended,
a woman's skull in pieces,
a boy,
a scream spilling
truth

over the streets, the hills, consciousness.
Then spies invented, and conspiracies,
then back to dictionary-reading,
a new word learnt—*libre;*
and back again in those alleyways
of spies entrapped.
So many of us in Siberia
getting weapons,
hunting them all,
hunting them…
Will the world clap our singing,
when Ukraine has nothing left to say

Abou Eternity

A reason for your death
I know not, but I answer,
"I know not,"
just as I know nothing,
even when I've seen your corpse,
little and slaughtered
over a street in your town;
I've seen your casket lowering
in the depths of soul,
in the gut unyielding
of Ukraine unshaken.
I might see you someday
upon time stretched
and again you'll ask me,
"Have you known my death yet?
how I stopped a tank with a toy riffle?"
As assassins asked me,
"Have you known your death yet?
And they were snow-strangers
from a far-off imperium
where strings are woven
in light's absence."
Again, "I know not,"
boy, I know not

why a common murderer
stepped over your shadow
as it walked the path
to school always taken.
Yet we learn from men,
to hope for what's better,
and yet I know not
why your body's been severed by hate,
and bullets,
I know not why your parents
will not see you someday,
will not feel you someday
inside your own eye's tenderness
or the lightness of laughing.
Oh, boy,
from a homeland so touched
by hate, by perversion,
by a faraway emperor
where snow is woven
in light's absence.
Sadness has its boundary
in the death of children,
so it is that common assassins
allow themselves to salivate fury,
drip over the depths of soul,
in the gut unyielding
of Ukraine unshaken.

So

So you've destroyed,
who then will love you?
So you've killed,
who then will love you?
Where will you settle?
Eat there
on the table
of the home of that family
whose child you've shot at?
Will someone dare knead your dough?
The hands of the mother
whose house you've blown over?
Who will you persuade
of your own goodness,
your acts of justice,
so sacred, eternal?
So it is that we've seen you
charge towards an old lady
who succumbed under infernal
weight of machinery.

Did you fear her?
I've noticed you avoid
one-on-one fighting,
that you shot from a distance,
unseen,
cowardly,
killer of innocence.
Are you a coward?
Are you the brave Russian
who enjoys burning houses
and judging those who survived it?
Well then, let's build from simple to complex,
today towards eternity,
so your intelligence
has no room for a question;
you'll understand then, my friend,
that this is serious.
Here it is: ancient code
where the guilt of the years
that you've taken from children
are sheltered in song.
Do you get it now, Russian?
Here's what you must decipher,
or be all-avoidant,
of that which pushes us humans
to hold sacred and share it.

Who will knead your dough?
Who will carry the weight
of crushing an old man?
You are here, now, in our history,
no more than a common murderer,
with no way out, my friend,
no way out
of the depths of a sin,
trapped in yourself
till a day where tombs open
and close at your fate.

Seven Words

Peace

Due to Civil War in El Salvador (1980–1992)
and its eighty thousand deaths.

Where is it, sunflower,
bones numb and hope broken,
dazed in time, sleepy
inside the cave of the millenary hill,
legacy broken and broken impulse,
the proud Chimera of your race?
From the depths of the milk it rises,
from an old mountain at the riverside;
from old hope a new longing
will dislocate as flame,
impossibly uncompromised life
and dilated war.
Sunflower, sunflower,
swollen chest,
drum and axe colored,

this death so unheard of
that will move the tyrant
and towards your deathbed
carry groans sustaining your uncertain name,
your blood's, your race's death
built up in frightened pleas.
Sunflower, sunflower,
let the wind blow
your lament, selfless and solitary,
cried today
for this homeland
consumed in murderous silence
imprinted in the sky,
cruel earth,
tame earth.
Sunflower, sunflower,
where does it come from,
this proud steam,
this suffocating mud destroying
all that's black and unhappy and feeds
that very evil that entraps itself
in the violent corner of your homeland?
Sunflower, sunflower,
with no shine
for the glowworm on the path of the elderly;
it cheers not the *zenzontle*
of the nooks of your age.
Sight tired,

Broken heart,
Mind boiling,
Stretched fingers,
Half-opened eyes,
Tired thigh,
Tired spirit:
This is the way I see you,
I can wait no more,
West Lord,
skin threaded
by sin dispersed in a thousand shreds;
let's fix your countenance,
paint your face,
let your body tremble,
get up
and acknowledge death, stunned,
as real,
in the mountains alive,
towns,
cities,
roads,
alive in the soul of your children.
Sunflower, sunflower,
evening serpent,
dreamy quetzal that dares not say
what time could teach us to follow.
Let your love for life
shine over us, pilgrim,

let it vanish the very earth from their belly,
the murderous bite of this war,
and let it bring hope skinny,
a breath of light,
a moment of peace.

Lightness

Yours will be the earth
and a flame from the sun,
and the secret of night,
and the blue pattern of an unending story
that starts in the shadows
and ends in the ulcer
of mercy.
You slow down your step to match the night;
you move closer to infamy and despair;
you grow your lineage
on shreds of a spell
that blames you, that searches
and mocks and feeds you;
on your way you leave
memories of each hour
filled by life
covering failure.
If you weren't beautiful
there would be no place
for your lineage
in the hidden evenings.
If you weren't beautiful,

your secret would be
no more than a shred of out-of-breath mourning,
with no music.
Old, winged being,
you who crowned the spirits,
who destroyed thousands of empires
with indecent magic;
Troya's battles are written
upon your breast
and as the fighting ends
heroes surrender to you.
Today's *pasionaria*,
tomorrow's stubbornness,
comb of tenderness,
envy of simpletons
who aren't fond of the battle
in which dreams are forged,
in which life has its beginning,
where man finally finds
some other heaven,
other way of being,
another universe.
Your name is Lightness;
the beauty that supports you
lifts multitudes
from their vacant sorrows,
their broken eagerness
and their sad faces.

Upon the light in your eyes
I can guess at the strength
that leads to forever;
the brush of your hands
can corrupt any wiseman,
magnify any poor man,
find a legend, there
where peace meets its ending.

Faith

Path of the spark,
striking path,
adhesion to eternity,
incongruous truth of all strangeness,
unusual and probable.
I am born in the darkness of impossibility
till I explode into meteors;
each one a hit
affirming that what was missing,
was after all there; the hand,
the boldness, the talent
that inspires respect
in God's eyes
and a willingness to follow
the strings and start
and finish the story.
Empires were born
from that dream I created;
inside me, science looks
to rest and rehearse,
and art to change,
to turn.
Virgin's eyes,
star's spark:

Everything inside me finds
decline, motive, and beginning.
Beauty is teacher,
eternity my right,
cause through me it escapes
from a mourning city
and a pain eternal;
cause through me they relate,
life and hope,
the peak of flame
that lights the universe.
In its frontier I define
fate in its elusiveness
and in their clothes delay
the shadow of death;
since I am faith,
poetry.

Truth

I must abandon, determined,
life and bolt;
follow the steps
of hope's blue lightning
when, headed towards skill and duty,
vision will leave its own resentment.
From God I'll expect a last chance at leisure,
a last glance at the path of sadness.
From this persistent turn, discordant,
unhappy and battered, I'll get crying;
to it I'll plead,
to it and the edge of fear,
determined by God and bolt:
Trust me not,
yesterday's broken mockery,
devoted shepherd, dream-eater,
steep labyrinth where fear takes cover,
I come here, defiant.
I come here, determined,
through a door that hides truth in dreaming,
I bring the darkened corner of misfortune,
the all-black hideout for compassion,
and the shiny grief of a thousand dead ones.

I am the maker,
life started
as my word began to walk;
without me there's no beyond,
I am the final dot to my own line,
the pregnant message of what's uncertain
which opens the curtain to eternity.
I am science,
I am envy and envy's plunder,
the altar for tomorrow,
the wrappings to the wind and the wind's melody,
the origin for music and a thief cunning,
hampa and tyranny.
The wisdom star has gone straight through me,
the oldest wound almost choked by me,
and time itself holds my cavities.
I am this and more, much more.
I can decipher the true name of water,
I can chain up the echo of number.
Inside me path and wilderness invented,
cities, stars and traveling reef.
I am the patricide rising,
law for the assassin
and a lullaby for children.
I am the abuser, the opportunist;
within myself was forged the courage
the cowardness, all vile crowned and proudly rising;
I've given names and land to all,

I've thrown them back their own embers
till they found their resting place inside me:
death of will, duty and unwillingness.
Without me there's no after,
my name is Truth,
my page is wind.
My name is Truth,
my page is wind.

Hope

Chirping nests inside me,
singing of what's to come,
its law and destiny,
the path towards ending.
Night tells me about
passing hours and tedium;
time about
mission and vigor.
I invented auction,
omen,
the slow, echoing
heavy
step of fate,
of infinite distance
where the end of it all
takes a nap
surrounded by knowledge
and sleep's vowels.
I am the given word
that leaves no sound behind
and the evasive look
of a distant lover
who might not come back;

the one who left the mapping
of a soul in the air,
there where a verse begins
to cave into mystery;
the one you wouldn't quit
following in silence
in the willingness to trap
between the lighted fence
that nourished your desire.
My name is Hope;
my step, my wings
encompass the horizon,
and even death
finds its amusement
and leaves the scythe
at my lintel,
here it tucks itself in,
and tells me, safe from the horizon
and all clustered ages,
about its passage through the road
of men, about martyrdom
when remembering the fierce
hole of its beginning.
Inside me
sadness stops crying.
Heaven's step and mercy
found in me the example.
My name is Hope.
I am God's voice,
I am His scepter.

Within me only truth,
I am men's essence,
God's essence,
I am His voice,
I am His scepter.

Belief

Because I am weak,
I can't increase
my own nourishment;
because I don't know
what's the limit of a word
or the light towards which
a thought travels;
because I know no origin
or ending;
because it never is
what it seems,
I can't go back
to what could be.
Because I am weak
I can't stand
the weight of silence
nor the bite of absence.
If I can't fly,
all that's left for me
is crying out
respect's consent
for what could have been.

Little being, fleeting,
you who walk the road
that contains your ending,
you cannot contain
nor detain
a second even
of what has been.
Because I am weak,
I peek in my memory
with not the slightest blink,
in an attempt to catch
the moment in which time stands,
and all remembrance
lights up
with genius's wick,
with the scream of the soul
that's escaping itself
and filling the distance
where time moves;
will of men,
will of genius.
I can't share with anyone
the suspicion raised
when I found the place
where prayer meets
the word impious
and eternal truth
where genius flourishes.

That's the very instance when
Supreme Goodness
can be guessed at
there where everything good has its origin,
where torturous secrets
are deciphered;
and from here till the beginning
or till my entrance's lintel
in the final line,
if someone still believes in me
it must be Him.

The Seventh Word

No name,
For you to write,
For you to call
and lead the steps
that we must follow.
The peaking form of saying
that protects those
who've been,
who'd written
those first words
that send us
on the path;
this that marks the direction
of colossal infancy
where the world exploded.
No more to say,
in it you will trap
the last prodigy,
the search's end,

the beginning
of it all: eternity.

About the Author

Renato Bettio (Dr. Roberto Arévalo Araujo MD, FACP) was born in El Salvador. After finishing high school, he traveled to Mexico to continue studying and graduated as a doctor and a surgeon from UNAM in 1970. He then worked at the Oakwood Hospital (Dearborn, MI) and at CMDNJ in New Jersey. There he also studied Hematology and Oncology as a subspecialty. He is Board Certified in Internal Medicine, as well as in Hematology and Oncology.

He is the founder of the Cancer and Hematology Center at Pasco County, Florida, a center that offers radiotherapy, immunotherapy, and chemotherapy. He is also a founder of the Medical Mission of Mercy / Medical Mission

International, whose goal is to take free medical, surgical, and ophthalmologic attention to homeless people east of El Salvador. This mission has been recognized by the Congress at El Salvador and was nominated for a Nobel Prize.

Now, he brings to you, dear reader, a piece of the inspiration his soul embraces. He writes stories about impunity and misery that affect his Central American fellow countrymen. Yet he also ascribes himself to the tangible faith of those affected. In them, in spite of their suffering, the longing for life doesn't go out; they have a philosophy that keeps them thinking that it's better to be.

Del origen de La Luz

ISBN Hardcover: 978-1-63765-624-2
ISBN Paperback: 978-1-63765-612-9

Este libro traza el camino de un sueño. El sueño empieza en la juventud del autor, expresado en los poemarios "Añoranzas" y "Ausencias".

El descrito parámetro, ceñido por la impotencia al contemplar la impunidad de falaces gobernantes y despiadados criminales, cebándose en la pobreza eterna de mi país, trata de sacudir el espíritu del lector en la historia "La Luz", en la cual se puede percibir, en sus últimos párrafos, la victoria de los ignorados, los de siempre. Esa victoria continúa en "El origen de La luz" con la descripción de un hallazgo inimaginable y capaz de cambiar el rumbo de la humanidad entera. Pero el hallazgo no será para unos pocos, es para todos los que albergan la nobleza en sus conductas y no se rige por la codicia, pues sólo obedece a los designios de la paz entre los pueblos. ¡Quién pudiera ser parte de este sueño!

"Las comadres" nos baja al trajín diario de nuestras gentes, quienes nos presentan sus ideas inmutables en el dejo de su esencia. Porque ellas son así, inmutables, porque advierten y conocen lo esencial.

El deleite innato en el poemario "Aventuras en poesía" es mi regalo para ti, que aún sueñas.